# The Wednesday Wars

Gary D. Schmidt

# TEACHER GUIDE

**NOTE:**

The trade book edition of the novel used to prepare this guide is found in the Novel Units catalog and on the Novel Units website. Using other editions may have varied page references.

Please note: We have assigned Interest Levels based on our knowledge of the themes and ideas of the books included in the Novel Units sets, however, please assess the appropriateness of this novel or trade book for the age level and maturity of your students prior to reading with them. You know your students best!

SBN 978-1-60878-716-6

opyright infringement is a violation of Federal Law.

2020 by Novel Units, Inc., St. Louis, MO. All rights reserved. No part of is publication may be reproduced, translated, stored in a retrieval system, or ansmitted in any way or by any means (electronic, mechanical, photocopying, cording, or otherwise) without prior written permission from Novel Units, Inc.

eproduction of any part of this publication for an entire school or for a school stem, by for-profit institutions and tutoring centers, or for commercial sale is rictly prohibited.

ovel Units is a registered trademark of Conn Education.

inted in the United States of America.

To order, contact your
local school supply store, or:

Toll-Free Fax: 877.716.7272
Phone: 888.650.4224
3901 Union Blvd., Suite 155
St. Louis, MO 63115

sales@novelunits.com

novelunits.com

# Table of Contents

# Skills and Strategies

## Critical Thinking
Compare/contrast, research, evaluation, brainstorming

## Comprehension
Identifying attributes, main idea, predicting, cause/effect, sequencing

## Writing
Essay, character sketch, journal, poetry, summary, newspaper article

## Listening/Speaking
Interview, oral presentation, discussion, dramatization

## Vocabulary
Definitions, synonyms/antonyms, parts of speech, context clues, glossary

## Literary Elements
Climax, figurative language, theme, character analysis, setting, point of view, genre, conflict, symbolism

## Across the Curriculum
Health/Sports—bullying, Vietnamese recipes, New York Yankees, camping, running; Science—architecture; Social Studies—the Vietnam War (especially the Battle of Khe Sanh), relief agencies, Jewish and Christian traditions, Martin Luther King, Jr., Robert F. Kennedy, political campaigns; Art—diorama, caricature; Literature—works of William Shakespeare, *Treasure Island*

**Genre:** fiction

**Setting:** Long Island, New York; 1967–1968

**Point of View:** first person

**Themes:** love, war, reconciliation, family, coming of age, peace, hope, success, perseverance, identity, friendship

**Conflict:** person vs. person, person vs. self

**Style:** narrative

**Tone:** candid, conversational, humorous

**Date of First Publication:** 2007

## Summary

In 1967 Long Island, seventh grader Holling Hoodhood is the only student in his class who does not attend Catechism or Hebrew School on Wednesday afternoons. Therefore, Mrs. Baker has him study Shakespeare, which Holling ultimately connects to his own life. Amidst classroom debacles, family crises, and political upheaval, Holling must navigate the seventh grade without getting "killed" by his classmates or disappointing his teacher. He must also avoid affecting the family business negatively. As Holling learns the value of freedom and the power of love over hate, he develops self-confidence and realizes that he can stand up to his father and follow his own path.

## About the Author

**Personal:** Gary D. Schmidt was born in Hicksville, New York in 1957. He grew up during the Vietnam War, much like the main character in *The Wednesday Wars*. He was raised Baptist and grew up with friends from school who were Irish Catholic or Jewish. This sometimes left him as the only Protestant kid in class. He was told at a young age that he was a poor reader, but one teacher worked with him on his reading and he eventually became a voracious reader and book collector. One of his favorite authors is Katherine Paterson, and one of his favorite books is *The Little World of Don Camillo* by Giovanni Guareschi, which inspired the school's name "Camillo Junior High" in *The Wednesday Wars*. Schmidt is a medievalist, a devoted husband, a father of six children, and an author of over 30 books.

**Education/Career:** Schmidt graduated from Gordon College in 1979, which was the same year he married his wife, Anne. Schmidt continued his education at the University of Illinois at Urbana-Champaign and received his M.A. in English in 1981 and his Ph.D. in medieval literature in 1985. Since then, he has taught English at Calvin College in Grand Rapids, Michigan. Schmidt's novel *Lizzie Bright and the Buckminster Boy* (2004) is a Michael L. Printz Honor book, and both this novel and *The Wednesday Wars* (2007) are Newbery Honor books. Schmidt later used the character Doug Swieteck as inspiration for *Okay for Now* (2011), a "spin-off" of *The Wednesday Wars*.

All rights reserved

# Characters

**Holling Hoodhood:** seventh grader; studies Shakespeare after school with Mrs. Baker; learns he can determine his own future; narrator of the story

**Danny Hupfer:** seventh grader; Holling's loyal best friend; prepares for his bar mitzvah

**Mrs. Betty Baker:** seventh-grade English teacher at Camillo Junior High; former Olympic medalist; teaches Holling Shakespeare; helps Holling with many obstacles he encounters

**Meryl Lee Kowalski:** seventh grader; teases Holling because she likes him romantically

**Mr. Hoodhood:** Holling's strong-willed father; architect and owner of Hoodhood and Associates; Chamber of Commerce Businessman of 1967; uninterested in his children's lives unless it affects his business

**Mrs. Hoodhood:** Holling's passive mother; always agrees with her husband and acquiesces to his wishes

**Heather Hoodhood:** Holling's older sister; clashes with her father; eventually runs away but returns home

**Paul Kowalski:** Meryl Lee's father; owner of Kowalski and Associates, a rival architecture firm

**Mrs. Bigio:** Camillo Junior High's cafeteria worker; excellent pastry chef; husband is killed in Vietnam

**Mai Thi Huong:** seventh grader; Vietnamese refugee who lives at the Catholic Relief Agency

**Doug Swieteck:** seventh-grade troublemaker; Holling's friend

**Doug Swieteck's brother:** eighth-grade bully; known for his daring antics

**Mr. Goldman:** local bakery owner; president of the Long Island Shakespeare Company

**Mr. Guareschi:** principal of Camillo Junior High; referred to as a "dictator"

**Mrs. Sidman:** administrator who becomes principal of Camillo Junior High after Mr. Guareschi is "reassigned"

**Mr. Vendleri:** Camillo Junior High's janitor

**Coach Quatrini:** track coach at Camillo Junior High

**Miss Violet:** nicknamed "Miss Violet of the Very Spiky Heels" by Danny Hupfer; choir teacher at Camillo Junior High

**Mr. Petrelli:** geography teacher at Camillo Junior High

**Lieutenant Tybalt Baker:** Mrs. Baker's husband; serving in Vietnam; declared missing in action

**Chit:** Heather's fellow "flower child" friend; drives a yellow Volkswagen Beetle; travels to California with Heather

**Mr. Bradbrook:** chairman of the school board

**Sycorax and Caliban:** Mrs. Baker's class's pet rats; escape into the walls of Mrs. Baker's classroom and are subsequently feared by students

All rights reserved

# Background Information

## Vietnam War

The Vietnam War began in 1954 and ended on April 30, 1975 with the fall of Saigon. Conflict arose between the Communist regime of North Vietnam and the Viet Cong (spelled "Vietcong" in the novel), its southern allies, and South Vietnam and the United States, its major ally, in an attempt to reunify the country after it was separated by the Geneva Accords. In 1965, President Lyndon B. Johnson sent U.S. ground troops into Vietnam after the Democratic Republic of Vietnam (North Vietnam) torpedo boats attacked two American ships in August 1964. In January 1968, North Vietnam surprised the U.S. and South Vietnam military with a brutal attack on hundreds of South Vietnamese cities and towns. President Richard M. Nixon began a process called "Vietnamization" to withdraw troops in 1969, but his efforts to stop the war also caused it to spread into Laos and Cambodia. This, in turn, caused increased public outrage in America. The last American troops returned home in 1973. In April 1975, North Vietnam captured South Vietnam and the country reunited as the Socialist Republic of Vietnam.

The Battle of Khe Sanh (spelled "Khesanh" in the novel) is mentioned repeatedly throughout *The Wednesday Wars*. It was the longest and most debated battle of the Vietnam War. American troops established a base close to Khe Sanh to monitor the Ho Chi Minh trail, block access to enemy forces from Laos, and act as a shelter for defense along the Demilitarized Zone. Shortly after the base was established, the Communist forces from North Vietnam increased their number of troops around Khe Sanh. Some argue that the North Vietnamese's attacks on Khe Sanh were a diversion to distract American troops from the Tet Offensive, in which North Vietnamese launched a large-scale attack on hundreds of cities in South Vietnam. Others argue that the Communist forces intended to seize the combat base because of its position and the large number of troops sent to the Khe Sanh area. The battle lasted over 70 days and involved approximately 6,000 American troops and allies and 20,000 North Vietnamese soldiers. Eventually, the Americans gained control as North Vietnam pulled back. By June 1968, American troops had gained mobile control of this area of South Vietnam, and the base at Khe Sanh was abandoned after the troops were evacuated.

**Note:** Some people refer to the fighting in Vietnam as the "Vietnam Conflict," since the U.S. never officially declared war on Vietnam. Other people believe that the use of the term "war" is accurate because war is defined as two factions fighting violently against one another. Many also believe that the refusal to refer to the Vietnam War as such is to discredit the soldiers who fought valiantly on behalf of the South Vietnamese.

## Robert F. Kennedy

Robert Francis "Bobby" Kennedy was born on November 20, 1925, in Brookline, Massachusetts. He was the seventh of nine children born to Joseph and Rose Kennedy. Robert Kennedy grew up to be well-educated and a happily married husband and devoted father. In 1960, he managed the presidential campaign for his brother, John F. Kennedy. He became the Attorney General and was respected for his nonpartisan efforts. He was also a close friend and advisor to his brother (e.g., he played a key role in the development of the Civil Rights Act of 1964 and helped make foreign policy decisions during the Cuban Missile Crisis).

After John F. Kennedy's assassination, Robert Kennedy resigned as Attorney General and became a New York Senator. As a United States Senator, he continued to work on behalf of poor, disabled, and powerless Americans.

All rights reserved

At the time of his election, Robert Kennedy supported the American policies in Vietnam. But by 1966, he began speaking out against the Johnson Administration. In 1968, he announced his candidacy for the presidency. He focused his campaign on bringing hope to war-weary Americans. He won critical primary races but was assassinated on June 5, 1968, in Los Angeles, California at age 42.

**William Shakespeare**

William Shakespeare was born in Stratford-upon-Avon. He was purportedly born in 1564 and his birth date is observed on April 23. He likely learned Latin and Greek and read Roman literature during his schooling. At age 18, he married Anne Hathaway, with whom he had two daughters, Susanna and Judith, and one son, who died at a young age.

Shakespeare was a poet and playwright for some of the most famous audiences of his time. Common themes emerge in Shakespeare's works, including the passing of time and the far-reaching power of love and beauty. Shakespeare's 30-plus plays are often divided into four categories: histories, comedies, tragedies, and romances. Some of his most famous works include *Henry VI, Romeo and Juliet, Julius Caesar, Hamlet, Othello, King Lear, Macbeth,* and *The Tempest.*

Shakespeare passed away on April 23, 1616, months after he wrote his will in January 1616. His works have endured throughout the centuries. Many attribute this to the beauty of his writings and the universality of the themes therein.

## Initiating Activities

Use one or more of the following to introduce the novel.

1. Brainstorming: Have the class brainstorm about the concept of "war" using the Attribute Web on page 33 of this guide.

2. History: Discuss the Vietnam War with the class. Ask students: Who was President of the United States at the time? How did Americans feel about America's involvement in the war? Why?

3. Social Studies: Hold a classroom discussion about bullying. Ask students: What defines a bully? How should victims of bullying respond?

4. Research: Instruct students to research bar mitzvahs. Have them answer the following questions: What is the purpose of the celebration? When does it occur?

5. History: Have students research the life and writings of William Shakespeare. As a class, discuss why his writing is still relevant and popular today.

6. Debate: Facilitate a class debate over whether love or war has the most power. Have students use critical thinking to develop logical arguments to support their positions.

All rights reserved

 © Novel Units, Inc.

# Vocabulary Activities

1. Start/Stop: Divide the class into two teams. One person from each team will stand at one end of the room. Each team is given a vocabulary word at random, which they must define without assistance. If that team can define the vocabulary word, their standing teammate may move forward one step and then stop. If the team answers incorrectly, the opposing team's standing member may move forward two steps. The team whose standing teammate reaches the opposite side of the room first wins.

2. Word Quilt: Have students create a word quilt. Each student will choose a vocabulary word from the lists in this guide. Using different colors of paper, have each student create eight unique squares to represent the word they chose—definition, part of speech, pronunciation, a simile, an antonym, a sentence, an illustration, and a quote from the novel. Finally, have students paste their squares together on a larger square sheet of paper. Display the word quilts in the classroom.

3. Glossary: Ask students to keep a list of unfamiliar or difficult words they encounter while reading the novel. Then, have each student create a glossary from their list. Glossaries should be alphabetized and include each word's page number, part of speech, and definition as it is used in the novel.

4. Vocabulary Squares: Select nine students to sit in three rows of three in the classroom. Give each student a large cut-out of an X and an O. Select two other students to compete. One student is "X," and the other is "O." Student X is asked to define a vocabulary word. S/he must choose one of the nine students sitting in a square to define the word and then state whether s/he agrees or disagrees with the given definition. If Student X correctly agrees or disagrees with the given definition, the sitting student displays the X. If Student X incorrectly agrees or disagrees, the sitting student displays the O. Alternate turns between Students X and O. The first student to have three Xs or Os in a row (vertical, horizontal, or diagonal) is the winner.

5. Word Chain: Divide the class into groups, and give each group the same set of 15 vocabulary words. The group must write each word and its definition on a separate sheet of paper. Then, they must think creatively to connect the sheets of paper together to form a chain. There must be a reason why each word is connected to the next. Reasons may be as varied as they both "start with j," "describe the main character," or "relate to politics." Have students write the reasons at the bottom of each sheet of paper as they connect them. The group with the longest chain is the winner. Display word chains in the classroom.

All rights reserved

# September

Holling Hoodhood, the only Presbyterian in Camillo Junior High's seventh grade, believes that his teacher Mrs. Baker hates him. While the rest of his class leaves early on Wednesdays for Hebrew School or Catechism, Holling is left alone with Mrs. Baker. After school, Holling goes home to the "Perfect House" where he lives with his sister, mother, and father. His father is an architect—a perfectionist concerned mainly with upholding his reputation and that of his company, Hoodhood and Associates. While avoiding a collision with Doug Swieteck's brother during a soccer game at recess, Holling accidentally trips him and spoils what he believes is Mrs. Baker's plan for his (Holling's) demise. He maintains that Mrs. Baker resents him when he learns she is recommending he retake his previous math course.

| Vocabulary |
| --- |
| parishioners |
| mutilation |
| alternating |
| ally |
| emporium |
| recruited |
| perimeter |
| foil |
| propulsion |
| accomplice |
| negligent |
| mooring |

## Discussion Questions

1. Why does Holling think Mrs. Baker "hates" him? Why does he seek an "ally"? *(Holling believes Mrs. Baker hates him because of the look he receives after she finds out he will stay with her on Wednesday afternoons when the other students leave for Hebrew School or Catechism. He believes an ally will help him defend himself against Mrs. Baker.)*

2. What is the setting of the novel? Which characters have been introduced so far? How does the author begin to develop the characters? *(The novel is set in Long Island, New York during the Vietnam War. Holling is the main character and narrator of the text, so readers gain insight into his personality and beliefs. Mrs. Baker, Doug Swieteck's brother, and Holling's family are also introduced. Holling's search for an ally yields descriptions of each new character. Holling's father, for instance, cares mostly about his work and image in the community. Holling's mother is compassionate but passive, while Holling's sister seems to be a typical older sister.)*

3. Why doesn't Holling want to go outside for recess? Why does he eventually leave the classroom? *(Holling believes that Mrs. Baker has orchestrated a plot against him and recruited Doug Swieteck's delinquent brother to help her. Holling eventually goes outside for recess because Mrs. Baker insists, and he suspects he'd also be in danger if he stayed alone with her.)*

4. Describe the conflict that emerges between Holling and Doug Swieteck's brother. How is the conflict resolved? *(Doug Swieteck's brother persuades Holling to join the soccer game, assigning Holling to the opposite team. As soon as Doug Swieteck's brother gains possession of the ball, he runs straight toward Holling while trying to score a goal. Holling decides to stand his ground by the goal but moves out of the way at the last second, inadvertently causing Doug Swieteck's brother to trip and fly headfirst into the goal post. The conflict is resolved when Doug Swieteck's brother must leave school for ten days for medical observation, eliminating new immediate threats to Holling's well-being.)*

5. What is the meaning of the sentence Mrs. Baker gives Holling to diagram? Why do you think she gives Holling a more difficult sentence than his classmates? *(Answers will vary. The sentence means that people take good things for granted and don't realize their value until they are gone. Some students might think Mrs. Baker gives Holling this sentence out of spite, but other students might think she is trying to challenge him to work harder.)*

All rights reserved

6. Why does Mr. Guareschi call Holling into his office? How does Mrs. Baker respond to the outcome of this meeting? *(Mrs. Baker has recommended that Holling retake his previous math course on Wednesday afternoons at 1:45 p.m. Mr. Guareschi calls Holling into his office to review this request and decides that since Holling already passed the course he doesn't need to retake it. Mrs. Baker finds the decision "regrettable.")*

7. What new information do readers discover about Mrs. Baker at the end of September? What does the author leave unanswered about Mrs. Baker's behavior toward Holling? Do you think Holling's belief that she "hates [his] guts" (p. 6) is rational? Why or why not? *(Mr. Guareschi announces that Mrs. Baker's husband will soon be deployed to Vietnam, but she has no visible reaction. The author never directly states whether Mrs. Baker likes or dislikes Holling. Answers will vary. Some students might think Holling is right to believe Mrs. Baker dislikes him and doesn't want him in class on Wednesday afternoons since she tries to reassign him to a different class. She may dislike him because she is forced to stay and teach only one student. Other students might believe Holling is over-dramatizing his teacher's feelings toward him.)*

8. **Prediction:** What will Mrs. Baker have Holling do on Wednesday afternoons?

## Supplementary Activities

1. Figurative Language: Begin keeping a chart of similes, metaphors, and examples of personification you find in the novel. Add to the chart as you read. Examples: **Similes**—"To ask your big sister to be your ally is like asking Nova Scotia to go into battle with you" (p. 8); "…there was a growl that rose out of him like he was some great clod of living earth that hadn't evolved out of the Mesozoic Era…" (p. 13); "…she makes me feel as stupid as asphalt" (p. 17); "The P.A. crackled and screeched like a parrot" (p. 18); "She kept her face as still as Mount Rushmore…" (p. 22).

2. Drama: Perform a sportscast with a partner describing the soccer game during recess.

3. Reading: Read a summary or review of *Treasure Island*. Then, write a paragraph telling why you would or wouldn't read the book. If you've already read it, explain whether or not you liked the book.

All rights reserved

# October

Holling and Mrs. Baker settle into a Wednesday afternoon routine, which involves Holling cleaning the classroom to pass the time. Mrs. Baker tells Holling to bring the cream puffs that Mrs. Bigio made for her up to the classroom, and when Holling's classmates see them they threaten to hurt him if he gets to eat one. While Holling is cleaning the chalkboard erasers outside, the chalk dust contaminates the cream puffs, which are sitting by the open window. Holling doesn't eat the one he is given, but his classmates still demand that he buy them cream puffs. Holling's father becomes upset when his daughter claims she is a flower child. Holling and Mrs. Baker begin reading Shakespeare's *The Merchant of Venice*, but not before Holling accidentally frees both pet rats while cleaning their cage.

| Vocabulary |
| --- |
| vile |
| quivering |
| reckon |
| unbecoming |
| equation |
| circulate |
| expel |
| presume |
| rioted |
| remnants |
| mercy |

## Discussion Questions

1. Who is Mai Thi, and where must she go on Wednesday afternoons? *(Mai Thi is a Vietnamese refugee brought to America by the Catholic Relief Agency. Because the agency is taking care of her, she is required to go to Catechism on Wednesday afternoons even though she is not Catholic.)*

2. What does Mrs. Baker have Holling do on Wednesday afternoons in October, and why? How does Holling behave during these afternoons? What does this indicate about his character? *(Holling cleans erasers, chalkboards, windows, and the Coat Room. He also removes cobwebs from the classroom ceiling and puts up Mrs. Baker's bulletin boards. Mrs. Baker assigns Holling these chores because she feels it would be pointless to teach him new material he would just hear again the next day. Holling never complains about the chores because he knows his father is currently competing with another architectural firm for a contract with the Baker Sporting Emporium, which belongs to Mrs. Baker's family. Answers will vary. Holling is obedient and doesn't want to cause trouble. He tries to keep everyone happy.)*

3. Who is Meryl Lee, and what does she think about Holling's theory that Mrs. Baker hates him? *(Meryl Lee is one of Holling's friends. Holling claims she told him she loved him in third grade, and he seems to like her, too. Meryl Lee believes that Holling is paranoid and that Mrs. Baker doesn't have a problem with him.)*

4. Why do you think Mrs. Baker chooses Holling to bring the cream puffs to her classroom? *(Answers will vary. After spending Wednesday afternoons with Holling, Mrs. Baker has learned more about him and has seen his responsible behavior. She obviously trusts him to safely move the cream puffs.)*

5. Whom do you think is at fault for the chalk-dusted cream puffs? Why? *(Answers will vary. Some students might think Holling is at fault, since the chalk dust came from the erasers he was cleaning outside. Other students might think Mrs. Baker is at fault for not closing the windows. Still others might think no one is to blame and that it was just an unfortunate accident.)*

6. Why is Mr. Hoodhood upset with his daughter? What does Mr. Hoodhood value, and what does his daughter value? *(Mr. Hoodhood's daughter tells him she is a "flower child," but he doesn't think highly of them. He says, "A flower child…is a hippie who lives in Greenwich Village in dirty jeans and beads and who can't change a pair of socks" [p. 36]. He is concerned that he will not be elected Chamber of Commerce Businessman of 1967 with a daughter who is a self-proclaimed flower child. Mr. Hoodhood values prestige and success. His daughter values peace and freedom of expression. In different ways, they both want to be a part of something bigger than themselves.)*

All rights reserved

7. How do cream puffs, rats, and Shakespeare play a role in Holling's life? *(Holling's classmates threaten to hurt him if he doesn't bring them all cream puffs, since they believe he ate one Mrs. Baker gave him. Then, as Holling's last chore, Mrs. Baker has him clean out the pet rats' cage, but he accidentally facilitates their escape into the school's walls. After the rat incident, Holling begins studying Shakespeare with Mrs. Baker, and while he believes she intends to bore him to death, he finds* The Merchant of Venice *interesting.)*

8. How do Holling's cream-puff dilemma, the escaped pet rats, and the beginning of his Shakespeare study impact the story? *(Answers will vary. Each incident is part of the story's rising action. Holling's conflict with his classmates over the cream puffs creates suspense about whether Holling will be able to get the cream puffs and what will happen if he doesn't. Readers will wonder if the rats will ever be captured, and the introduction of Shakespeare gives the author an opportunity to connect Holling's life with the lives of Shakespeare's characters from centuries ago.)*

9. According to Holling's analysis of Shylock on page 48 of the novel, which character in the novel might Shylock parallel? Explain. *(Answers will vary. Since Holling explains that Shylock is trapped into being someone he doesn't want to be, some students may think Shylock parallels Holling, who must behave perfectly because his father intends for him to inherit Hoodhood and Associates. Others may think Shylock parallels Mr. Hoodhood, who may feel he must adopt a certain attitude and maintain a certain image to stay successful. Still others may think Shylock parallels Holling's sister, who is unable to express herself the way she wishes and must conform to what her father expects a dutiful daughter should be.)*

10. **Prediction:** How will Holling afford the cream puffs for Mrs. Baker's class?

## Supplementary Activities

1. Figurative Language: Continue adding to your figurative language chart. Examples: **Similes**—"a breeze as gentle as a breath" (p. 28); "a scent that lingered like the smell of a dead animal caught underneath the floorboards" (p. 29); **Personification**—"...the world still hadn't let out its breath" (p. 36).

2. History: Research the efforts of relief agencies during the Vietnam War. Why did they bring children from Vietnam to the United States? What happened to these children once the war ended? Write a brief report detailing your findings.

3. Literature: Read a summary of *The Merchant of Venice*. Who are Shylock, Portia, and Antonio? Write a character sketch for these three characters based on your research.

All rights reserved

# November

Holling's father becomes frustrated with the problems arising in the "Perfect House." Holling memorizes and practices curses from Shakespeare's plays. Hoodhood and Associates acquires the Baker Sporting Emporium contract, and Mr. Hoodhood is elated. Holling agrees to participate in the Long Island Shakespeare Company's Holiday Extravaganza in exchange for a discount on two dozen cream puffs. The rats eat the cream puffs, but Mrs. Baker replaces them. Holling must reread *The Tempest*. Mrs. Bigio's husband dies in Vietnam, and people become more agitated about the Vietnamese refugees living in their community.

| Vocabulary |
| --- |
| rhythm |
| devious |
| jesting |
| swathe |
| coagulated |
| advance |
| virtue |
| rivalry |
| vandals |

## Discussion Questions

1. How is the "Perfect House" symbolic of Mr. Hoodhood's life? *(Answers will vary. Mr. Hoodhood works hard to maintain his pristine house. Similarly, he works hard to preserve his image in the community to receive awards and honors that will help him maintain his successful business. However, the Perfect House has imperfections [e.g., a leaky roof, mold, overflowing gutters] that taint its appearance over time. Mr. Hoodhood's family life is also imperfect. He disapproves of his daughter's political activism, and he pressures Holling to be perfect to prove he is worthy of inheriting the family company. In contrast, Mr. Hoodhood's children value the future of Hoodhood and Associates much less than their father.)*

2. Why does Holling appreciate *The Tempest*? Why do you think Mrs. Baker assigns Holling this play even though it contains mature content? *(Holling enjoys reading* The Tempest *because of its attempted murders, witches, wizards, monster, and cursing. Answers will vary. Some students might think the play is one of Mrs. Baker's favorites since her classroom's pet rats are named after the play's villains, Caliban and Sycorax. Other students might think Mrs. Baker considers Holling mature enough to read it and she is trying to challenge him.)*

3. What does Holling do with the curses he learns while reading *The Tempest*, and why? *(Holling practices the curses in front of his dresser mirror every night after dinner. He practices without his shirt because he thinks he looks more "menacing." Holling doesn't think it's important whether he understands the curses but rather that "It's all in the delivery..." [p. 50]. He also practices at school and creates his own combinations of curses. Answers will vary. He might want to use them on certain people if they upset him, or he might just be amused by the style of the language. The curses might also make him feel "powerful" when he might otherwise feel helpless in his life.)*

4. How do Meryl Lee and Holling interact during choir class? What does this indicate about their relationship? *(Meryl Lee teases Holling about singing soprano, and he uses one of his combined curses on her, infuriating her even more. Then, when Miss Violet accuses Meryl Lee of flirting with Holling, she becomes very embarrassed. Answers will vary. Although they tease each other and it seems like they dislike each other, Meryl Lee cares about how Holling treats her. She most likely has a crush on him.)*

5. How is Holling's cream-puff dilemma resolved? What new dilemma arises? Do you think Holling's classmates' demands are fair? Why or why not? *(Since Holling has been studying Shakespeare, he agrees to help Mr. Goldman by performing in the Long Island Shakespeare Company's Holiday Extravaganza for a discount on the cream puffs he needs for his classmates. When Holling brings the cream puffs to school, Mrs. Baker orders the class to go to recess before eating them, and when they return they find the rats eating the pastries. Answers will vary. Discussion can include the definition of justice. Some students might think it is unjust for the class*

All rights reserved

*to stay angry with Holling for something that was not his fault. These students might think Holling already tried his best by bringing in the cream puffs, and for the class to demand more [especially within ten days] is not reasonable.)*

6. How does Holling relate to Mrs. Baker's lesson on *The Tempest*? *(Answers will vary. When Holling can only deliver five cream puffs to the class, he feels defeated and "doomed." In Mrs. Baker's lesson after school, she says that defeat helps a person grow, but Holling disagrees and believes that defeat is simply defeat. Mrs. Baker tries to give Holling a different perspective to convey what she means. She tells Holling that everyone has a bad side, which is portrayed through Caliban, but she also believes that people can become better. Since Caliban symbolizes humanity, Mrs. Baker says she would have liked the play to show how people can rise above others' expectations of them. But Holling continues to believe that defeat is "just defeat.")*

7. What does Mrs. Baker mean when she tells Holling "the quality of mercy is not strained" (p. 71)? *(Just as Portia from Shakespeare's* The Merchant of Venice *saves Antonio with these words, Mrs. Baker is showing Holling compassion by helping him reach his own happy ending.)*

8. What devastating news does Mrs. Bigio receive? How does it affect the plot in the novel? *(Mrs. Bigio's husband is found dead in Vietnam. Shortly after the news spreads, the Catholic Relief Agency is vandalized, with the words "GO HOME VIET CONG" [p. 72] written across the front. Holling begins to draw connections from Shakespeare to the current situation. He says that Shakespeare is wrong because, based on Holling's reality, "sometimes the quality of mercy is strained" [p. 72].)*

9. **Prediction:** How will Holling's performance in the Shakespeare play affect his life?

## Supplementary Activities

1. Figurative Language: Continue adding to your figurative language chart. Examples:
   **Similes**—"…the stain was as wide as a garbage can lid…" (p. 49); "And I remembered the death threats hanging over me like Shylock's knife hanging over Antonio's chest" (p. 61);
   **Metaphor**—corrections Mrs. Baker makes to students' essays: a red plague (p. 54);
   **Personification**—"The azaleas…were half-naked and embarrassed…" (p. 49); "It looked like my test was bleeding to death" (p. 60).

2. Poetry: Write a poem about justice and/or happy endings.

All rights reserved

# December

Everyone in the school decorates for the winter holidays except for Mrs. Baker. Holling's Shakespeare performance is on the same night as Mickey Mantle's visit to the local sporting goods store. Holling is refused an autograph by the baseball legend because he is dressed in his yellow tights from the play. After witnessing this, Danny returns his autographed baseball to Mantle. Mrs. Bigio's grief from her husband's death causes her to speak rudely to the students, especially Mai Thi. Mrs. Baker arranges for Holling, Danny, and Doug to meet Joe Pepitone and Horace Clarke.

| Vocabulary |
| --- |
| seclusion |
| menorah |
| exquisite |
| vocation |
| corresponding |
| bribe |
| suspicion |
| insubstantial |
| revels |
| careened |
| crooning |

## Discussion Questions

1. Why do you think Mrs. Baker refuses to decorate for the holidays? Why isn't Holling in a "happy holiday spirit" (p. 75)? *(Answers will vary, but students should note that Mrs. Baker's husband is currently fighting in Vietnam. Holling is unhappy about playing the role of Ariel the Fairy in the upcoming Shakespeare production. He is even unhappier that his costume consists of yellow tights with white feathers on the seat.)*

2. What redeems the holidays for Holling? How does Mrs. Baker seem to feel about the event? *(Mrs. Baker announces that Mickey Mantle is going to be signing baseballs at the Baker Sporting Emporium. Mrs. Baker does not seem as enamored of the idea as her students. She would rather her students attend the Shakespeare performance and entices them to go by promising extra credit to anyone who attends.)*

3. How does Holling describe his role as Ariel to Meryl Lee, Mai Thi, and Danny? How does Mai Thi feel about his role? Why do you think she feels as she does? *(Holling tells his classmates Ariel is a warrior and he will be fighting rebels, omitting that Ariel is actually a fairy. He gives the impression that he will be wearing armor rather than tights. Mai Thi disapproves of Holling's role as a warrior. Answers will vary. Mai Thi might not like the idea of violence, since she has been displaced from her home country because of the war in Vietnam. She might also disapprove because she sees the hate war inspires in people.)*

4. How does Holling feel about his parents missing his performance? Why do you think he reacts this way? *(Holling seems to be hurt because after realizing that Danny's parents are in the crowd and his parents are not, he says, "And I guess you can't look out stage peepholes very long, because your eyes start to water, and the stuff in your nose gets drippy..." [p. 85]. Answers will vary. Based on Holling's parents' lack of attention toward their son thus far, some students might think he casually expresses his disappointment because he isn't too surprised they aren't there. Holling's easygoing and comical personality [even in difficult times] is also witnessed by his reaction.)*

5. What obstacles does Holling encounter on his way to meet Mickey Mantle? *(After the play is over, Holling sneaks to the dressing room to change. Finding the door locked, he throws a cape over his costume. He rushes outside to meet his father, but his father is not there. Holling then boards a bus and persuades the driver to take him to the Emporium for free. He realizes he doesn't have his baseball when he arrives, but the bus driver gives him one that was left on the bus. When Holling finally meets Mickey Mantle he is refused an autograph because of his costume.)*

All rights reserved

6. How does Danny react to Mickey Mantle's refusal to sign Holling's baseball? What does this indicate about Danny's character? *(Danny gives his signed baseball back to Mantle, calls him a "pied ninny," and walks away with Holling. Answers will vary. Danny shows that he is sympathetic and willing to sacrifice for his friends. He also shows that he judges people by their actions and not just by fame or celebrity.)*

7. What does Holling mean when he talks about gods dying inside people? *(Answers will vary. The "death" Holling is referring to is the metaphorical death of his and Danny's idol, Mickey Mantle. Both boys are distraught that one of their baseball heroes is not what they expected.)*

8. Whom do Holling, Danny, and Doug meet after school one day? Why does Mrs. Baker arrange this meeting? What does this indicate about her character? *(Mrs. Baker arranges for the boys to meet Joe Pepitone and Horace Clarke, two popular Yankees players. Answers will vary. Mrs. Baker heard about the incident with Mickey Mantle from her brother-in-law and most likely felt bad for them. Mrs. Baker might be trying to restore the boys' interest in baseball and their faith in their heroes, which was dashed when they met Mantle.)*

9. **Prediction:** What trials might the new year bring for Holling?


## Supplementary Activities

1. Figurative Language: Continue adding to your figurative language chart. Examples: **Similes**—"...Morning Announcements were as exciting as December drizzles..." (p. 73); "white linen cloth as huge as History" (p. 74); "hands as large as shovels, and...forearms... strong as stone" (p. 91); "hamburgers...cooked as thin as a record" (p. 94)

2. Social Studies: Holling's school celebrates both Hanukkah and Christmas. Use the Venn Diagram on page 34 of this guide to compare and contrast the two holidays.

3. History/Sports: Research Mickey Mantle, Joe Pepitone, or Horace Clarke. Write an essay that includes answers to the following questions: When did he play baseball? What position did he play? What did he do during his baseball career to make him well-known?

All rights reserved

## January

Doug Swieteck's brother posts copies of a newspaper photo of Holling as Ariel all over the school. Doug Swieteck's brother gives Doug a black eye for refusing to help him. Holling and his sister argue about Holling's future. It snows overnight, but the school stays open. Mr. Guareschi sends a memo to all teachers stating that all students must take the New York State Standardized Achievement Tests, despite bad weather conditions. Holling gets revenge on Doug Swieteck's brother by hitting him in the face with a snowball. Doug Swieteck's brother and his friends are about to retaliate when an out-of-control bus almost hits Holling's sister. Holling saves her and gets hit instead. The newspaper prints a picture of Holling rescuing his sister, and someone posts it around the school.

| Vocabulary |
| --- |
| splayed |
| impressive |
| intercepted |
| ample |
| nifty |
| fortifying |
| consonant |
| heath |
| eaves |
| thermal |
| vengeance |
| component |
| aerial |
| caches |

### Discussion Questions

1. What does the New Year's Eve edition of the *Home Town Chronicle* include an article about? What does Doug Swieteck's brother do with it? *(The New Year's Day newspaper edition includes a large photo of Holling as Ariel the Fairy "flying high in the air" [p. 101] on the front page. The headline reads, "Holling Hoodhood as Ariel the Fairy Soars Onstage to Rescue His Potent Master" [p. 103]. Doug Swieteck's brother sees the photo, steals the front page of the newspaper from people's porches, and then cuts the photo and headline out of each newspaper. He then paints each picture with yellow paint and plasters them all over Camillo Junior High. When Holling thinks that all the pictures have been removed, Doug Swieteck's brother continues to post them on Friday, Monday, and Tuesday. On Tuesday evening, Holling's sister informs him that the pictures were also posted in her high school.)*

2. What did Doug's brother do to him after he refused to help paint the pictures? Why do you think Doug refused to help? *(Doug's brother gave him a black eye. Answers will vary. Doug was being a loyal friend to Holling. Doug most likely considers Holling a good friend and therefore wants to protect him.)*

3. How does Holling respond to Doug's brother's actions? How would you react? *(Although Holling feels humiliated, saying, "...I figured this would be my last day at Camillo Junior High" [p. 104], he doesn't immediately respond. Answers will vary.)*

4. What does Mrs. Baker think about the newspaper photos? How does Holling offend her? *(Mrs. Baker thinks it is "a wonderful picture of [Holling] playing a wonderful part" [p. 109]. She tells Holling that people will soon forget about his performance as Ariel. Holling gets frustrated with Mrs. Baker and thoughtlessly insinuates that she has a carefree life. She is offended at his insensitivity, since her husband is currently fighting in Vietnam and she worries for his safe return every day.)*

5. When explaining *Macbeth*, Mrs. Baker claims Shakespeare is showing "that pride combined with stubbornness can be disaster" (p. 109). How might this statement apply to Mr. Guareschi? *(Answers will vary. Mr. Guareschi refuses to close the school when it snows and the roads ice over, forcing the buses to continue running and all teachers and students to attend school for the standardized tests. Then, everyone must endure the freezing temperature inside the school since the electricity is out. Another more indirect consequence of Mr. Guareschi's stubbornness is that Holling is hit by an out-of-control bus while trying to save his sister. Mr. Guareschi also refuses to admit that Sycorax and Caliban have escaped into the school's walls.)*

All rights reserved

6. How does Holling get revenge on Doug Swieteck's brother? Was this a good choice? Why or why not? *(Holling hits Doug Swieteck's brother in the face with a snowball. Answers will vary. Some students might think Holling deserved to get revenge. Other students might believe it was not a good idea because Doug's brother now wants revenge on Holling. Still other students might argue that Holling is making the situation worse because he is mirroring and encouraging Doug's brother's pattern of bad behavior.)*

7. Is it surprising that Holling's parents do not rush to the hospital after the bus accident? What do Mrs. Baker and Mr. Guareschi's actions indicate about them? *(Answers will vary. Some students might be surprised because of the gravity of the accident. They might think that any parent would be frantic to be at their child's side. Other students might not be surprised since Holling's parents have been absent from other significant events in his life, such as the Shakespeare play and Mickey Mantle appearance. Mrs. Baker shows how much she cares about Holling by driving him to and waiting at the hospital. Mr. Guareschi might wait with Holling because he cares about him or because he does not want to suffer liability for Holling's injury. Both show a great amount of care and compassion toward Holling.)*

8. Holling compares himself to Malcolm, the son of the murdered king in *Macbeth*, who has no more need for vengeance after Macbeth is killed and he finally becomes king. Why do you think Holling no longer feels a need for revenge on Doug's brother? Who in Holling's life can be compared to Macbeth, the power-hungry enemy of Malcolm? *(Answers will vary. Since Holling was photographed "flying high in the air" [p. 128] to save his sister and those photos were posted throughout his school, Holling probably feels that his reputation has been saved. Doug Swieteck's brother represents Macbeth because he is Holling's enemy.)*

9. **Prediction:** How will Holling's relationship with his sister change as a result of the bus incident?

## Supplementary Activities

1. Figurative Language: Continue adding to your figurative language chart. Examples: **Similes**—"working through Parts of Speech like I was Robert Louis Stevenson" (p. 118); "his words hovering like the snow in the air" (p. 122); "stood in line like a platoon" (p. 123); "snowballs as big as bowling balls" (p. 123); **Personification**—"...the wind sculpted the snow first into low mounds and then into strange, sharp shapes. And when the wind was finished with the snow, it threw itself against our house..." (p. 114).

2. Journal: From Doug Swieteck's brother's point of view, write what he thinks about covering the school in pictures of Holling in yellow tights.

3. Poetry: Write an acrostic poem using the word "revenge."

All rights reserved

# February

The Hoodhood family attends the ceremony for the Chamber of Commerce Businessman of 1967 Award, which is presented to Mr. Hoodhood. Holling studies *Romeo and Juliet* and asks Meryl Lee out for Valentine's Day. Holling's father is confident he will get the new junior high school contract, which will end Meryl Lee's father's business. Mrs. Bigio gives Holling her season tickets to the *Romeo and Juliet* production. After the play, Holling takes Meryl Lee to Woolworth's, where he unintentionally shares his father's design for the new junior high. Mr. Kowalski presents a modified design to the school board that reflects Mr. Hoodhood's modern elements, which enrages Mr. Hoodhood. Holling and Meryl Lee reconcile, and Mrs. Baker finds out her husband is missing in action.

| Vocabulary |
| --- |
| dank |
| lapel |
| prosperous |
| tragic |
| eternal |
| arrogant |
| unsavory |
| allotted |
| procedural |
| begrudge |

## Discussion Questions

1. How do Holling and his sister feel on the night of their father's award ceremony? *(Answers will vary. They complain about wearing a flower on their clothes, and Holling seems to feel that his father is undeserving of such a prestigious award because of the severity of his father's critical nature of the general business atmosphere. Holling's sister seems frustrated because she must act like the "perfect daughter" for the ceremony. She knows her father does not respect or care about her beliefs, so she defies him by flushing her flower down the toilet.)*

2. Contrast Holling's and Mrs. Baker's views of *Romeo and Juliet*. Why does Holling feel as he does? *(Holling thinks that both Romeo and Juliet are foolish, and the tone of his description of the story shows how silly he finds it. He calls it "stupid," while Mrs. Baker calls it "tragic and beautiful and lovely" [p. 135]. Holling thinks it's stupid because he claims Romeo and Juliet would have never killed themselves; they would have just ignored their parents and ran away together.)*

3. What problem does Holling face after he asks Meryl Lee out for Valentine's Day? What does he learn about the Kowalski family from his father, and how might this affect his relationship with Meryl Lee? What Shakespearean play does this relationship seem to reference? *(Holling has a small budget for his date with Meryl Lee, and he is worried she will think he is a "cheapskate." Holling's father tells him that the Kowalski firm will likely go out of business without the junior high school contract, and Meryl Lee will probably have to move. Meryl Lee and Holling's relationship parallels* Romeo and Juliet. *They are from opposing families, just as Romeo and Juliet were.)*

4. How is Holling able to take Meryl Lee to the *Romeo and Juliet* play? What else does he do for her? *(Mrs. Baker most likely told Mrs. Bigio about Holling's dilemma, so Mrs. Bigio gives Holling her season tickets to the performance. Holling gives Meryl Lee a rose, and after the play, Holling buys himself and Meryl Lee sodas at Woolworth's.)*

5. What do Meryl Lee and Holling discuss during their date? What does this discussion foreshadow? Do you think Meryl Lee intentionally brings up this topic? *(Meryl Lee and Holling discuss their fathers' designs for the new junior high school. Holling draws a picture of his father's design on his placemat, and Meryl Lee takes it as a souvenir. Answers will vary. Since readers are already aware of the pressure on Kowalski and Associates to get the junior high contract, they might infer that Mr. Kowalski will steal ideas from Holling's drawing of his father's design. Some students might think Meryl Lee always intended to steal Holling's father's plan. Other students might think she is just making conversation and venting.)*

All rights reserved

6. Discuss the ethics of Mr. Kowalski's decision to change his building design after seeing Mr. Hoodhood's design. *(Answers will vary. Some students might think it's okay that Mr. Kowalski changed his design since he didn't copy Mr. Hoodhood's entire plan, but other students might think it is still wrong since it was not Mr. Kowalski's idea to begin with.)*

7. Why does Mrs. Baker replace Holling's first *Romeo and Juliet* essay with the second? How is Holling applying the lesson Shakespeare teaches to his own life? *(Answers will vary. Mrs. Baker likely thinks Holling's second essay is a better interpretation of Shakespeare's work, since in Holling's second analysis he discusses the true meaning of love. After talking to Meryl Lee, Holling believes she didn't mean to hurt him. He realizes that she cares for him while simultaneously caring for her father and the success of his company. He decides to forgive her because he cares about her. Holling makes amends by bringing her a rose and a Coke.)*

8. Which architecture firm acquires the contract for the new junior high school, and why? Do you think Mr. Kowalski did the right thing? What does this indicate about his character? *(Hoodhood and Associates gets the contract because Kowalski and Associates withdraws its bid. Answers will vary. Some students might believe Mr. Kowalski made an ethical choice to withdraw, showing that he is honest and fair. He is not as ruthless as Holling's father, who calls Kowalski and Associates "chumps" and believes "if you can't play for keeps, you shouldn't be in the business in the first place" [p. 154].)*

9. How does Holling compare his father to Shylock from *The Merchant of Venice*? Why does Holling make this comparison? *(Holling compares his father to Shylock because his father might have become trapped into being someone other people expected him to be instead of following a different dream. Holling begins to question his father's motives after his father says, "...Kowalski never could play for keeps. And Hoodhood and Associates can" [p. 154]. Answers will vary. Holling might now believe his father is only maintaining his public image.)*

10. **Prediction:** How will the news about Lieutenant Baker ultimately affect Mrs. Baker's life?


## Supplementary Activities

1. Figurative Language: Continue adding to your figurative language chart. Examples: **Similes**— "each [model] covered with a white sheet, like they were some sort of national secret" (p. 146); "...the back of his neck grew as red as boiling sin..." (p. 147); "He rubbed his hands together like Shylock onstage"(p. 154); **Metaphor**—Mr. Bradbrook: God (p. 148)

2. Acting: Read a scene from *Romeo and Juliet,* and with a partner or group, reenact the scene for the class. (Note: The teacher should monitor the scene chosen for appropriateness.)

All rights reserved

# March

The fighting at Khesanh in Vietnam intensifies as American troops become trapped in trenches and bunkers while being bombarded by mortar shells. Mrs. Baker continues to teach normally, showing no concern about the war. It is announced that members of the school board are coming to observe Mrs. Baker's class and that tryouts for the varsity cross-country team will be on "the ides of March" (p. 162). Holling's sister and their father get into another political argument. Mrs. Baker teaches Holling how to run correctly, and Holling gives her some advice for the school board's visit. During the school board's visit to Mrs. Baker's classroom, the rats fall through the ceiling and Mrs. Sidman grabs them and puts them in a cage. The rats escape and chase Holling during his cross-country tryouts, but are killed when a bus runs over them. Holling makes the varsity team, and Mai Thi and Mrs. Bigio reconcile.

| Vocabulary |
| --- |
| refuse |
| unalloyed |
| underestimated |
| stance |
| unscathed |
| diction |
| dispense |
| demean |
| vanquished |
| dispatch |

## Discussion Questions

1. How does the war in Vietnam affect Holling's family? How does it seem to affect Mrs. Baker? Why does Mrs. Baker act this way? *(The Hoodhood family intently watches the news together in silence every night after dinner, without anyone arguing about politics. Holling says Mrs. Baker acts unaffected, "mov[ing] through [their] classroom as coolly as if Khesanh were just a proper noun in a sentence that needed to be diagrammed" [p. 157], and still demanding excellence from her students. Answers will vary. Mrs. Baker probably acts this way because she is trying to concentrate her attention on her students rather than the war, since her husband is currently missing and she does not want to be consumed by her fears and worries. Mrs. Baker might also not want to show weakness in front of her students.)*

2. Why is "the ides of March" (p. 162) significant? *(In the play, the ides of March is the day Julius Caesar was killed. It is also the day Mrs. Baker's class is observed by the school board and the day of cross-country tryouts. Holling is convinced that something awful will happen on this day as it does in* Julius Caesar.*)*

3. What does Mrs. Baker teach Holling to help him with cross country? What does Holling learn about Mrs. Baker as a result? Why do you think Mrs. Baker helps Holling? *(Mrs. Baker takes Holling to the track after school and teaches him how to run better. She coaches him on posture, arm and head position, and breathing patterns. As a result, he is able to run faster than Danny and many eighth graders. Holling learns that Mrs. Baker won a silver medal from the 1956 Olympics for running in the women's four-by-one hundred relay. Answers will vary. Mrs. Baker might help Holling because she knows he is nervous about the tryouts. When Mrs. Baker asks Holling about his preparation, he responds with, "Death, a necessary end…will come when it will come" [p. 167]. She might feel bad and want to help because she knows he is deserving and talented.)*

4. Why is Mrs. Baker upset that Holling only seems to care about the murders that occur in Shakespeare's plays? How can her summation of Shakespeare's messages relate to current events in 1967? *(Answers will vary. Mrs. Baker thinks the universal truths in Shakespeare's writings should not be belittled. She says Shakespeare emphasizes how love is more powerful than armies and fighting. Mrs. Baker might believe the President should heed Shakespeare's messages to end the war in Vietnam. A historical figure who also opposed violence was Martin Luther King, Jr. In 1967, he was leading peaceful protests demanding civil rights.)*

All rights reserved

5. How has Mrs. Sidman changed from the beginning of the novel? To what do you attribute these changes? *(Mrs. Sidman is more courageous and harder to rattle. At the beginning of the year, Doug Swieteck's brother played a prank on her, resulting in her reassignment to the Main Administrative Office where she hardly interacted with the students. Then she takes "a retreat in seclusion" [p. 73] in Connecticut and returns as a board member with newfound confidence, as evidenced by her reaction to the rats falling onto her lap in Mrs. Baker's classroom. Answers will vary.)*

6. How do the rats affect Holling's cross-country tryout? How do the rats die? *(The rats chase Holling after they escape from their cage. As a result, he runs faster than anyone and makes the varsity cross-country team. The rats are run over by a bus.)*

7. Compare and contrast Mrs. Baker's and Coach Quatrini's coaching techniques. *(Both Mrs. Baker and Coach Quatrini are direct and want Holling to do his best. Mrs. Baker helps him on an individual level, giving him more detailed guidance. She advises him on how to stand, how to position his arms and head, and how to breathe. Coach Quatrini trains all of the boys at one time and has them run around the track while he yells at them to go faster. He calls them "wimps" and "slugs," thinking that he is motivating them. He does not focus on the technical aspects of running as Mrs. Baker does.)*

8. How do Mrs. Baker and Mrs. Bigio support Mai Thi after an eighth grader is rude to her? How does Mrs. Bigio's behavior toward Mai Thi change, and why? How does the reconciliation between Mai Thi and Mrs. Bigio relate to Shakespeare? *(Mrs. Baker and Mrs. Bigio provide a Vietnamese dessert for the students in Mai Thi's class. Mrs. Bigio apologizes to Mai Thi for the way she treated her after her [Mrs. Bigio's] husband died. Answers will vary. After witnessing the eighth grader's hatred toward Mai Thi, Mrs. Bigio might have realized how unfair that kind of prejudice is and the pain Mai Thi is feeling. Mrs. Bigio and Mai Thi's reconciliation reflects Shakespeare's lesson that war is futile and people should choose love. The choice to love and support one another is life-giving and healing for both.)*

9. **Prediction:** How will Holling perform in his upcoming cross-country meets?

## Supplementary Activities

1. Figurative Language: Continue adding to your figurative language chart. Examples: **Similes**— "[The ceiling tiles] looked like sails in a full breeze" (p. 158); "Arms and legs like pistons" (p. 168); "teeth sinking into my heels like the assassins' daggers sinking into Caesar" (p. 179); **Metaphors**—Mrs. Baker's students: plants sprouting (p. 157); cross-country runners: "slugs" (p. 164); **Personification**—"...if a word can get worn out and die, this one died..." (p. 163); "my lungs screaming for air" (p. 164); "...the daffodils were playing their trumpets, and the lilacs were starting to bud and getting all giddy..." (p. 181).

2. Social Studies/Culture: Research popular foods in Vietnam. Select a recipe, and prepare a sample for the class.

3. Art: Draw a caricature of the rats during their escapade on the ides of March.

All rights reserved

# April

Mrs. Baker discovers that a mission is underway to rescue American military at Khesanh. Mrs. Sidman becomes principal of the school. Kowalski and Associates goes out of business, and Meryl Lee's family plans to move to her grandmother's house. The death of Martin Luther King, Jr. saddens people, and the nation is divided over the upcoming presidential race. Holling's father does not show up to take him to Opening Day at Yankee Stadium, so Mrs. Baker takes him instead. Holling's father and sister get into an argument about her future and her attending college after she graduates. Danny and Holling race in their first cross-country meet. Danny is in the lead until he runs into the woods and becomes injured. Holling listens to Mrs. Baker, passes the eighth graders, and wins the race.

| Vocabulary |
| --- |
| allusion |
| arteries |
| commuters |
| humane |
| contour |
| improper |
| scaffolding |
| levitate |
| brittle |

## Discussion Questions

1. Why do you think Mrs. Sidman replaces Mr. Guareschi as the school's principal? *(Answers will vary. The school board members may have believed Mr. Guareschi was not handling the problems at the school very well [e.g., the rats living in the walls and the bus accident involving Holling]. The way Mrs. Sidman handles the rat problem might have convinced the school board she is a better candidate for the job. They likely admire her problem-solving skills and resolve to reinstate her job after a much-needed break.)*

2. How does the upcoming presidential election further divide Mr. Hoodhood and his daughter? *(Mr. Hoodhood and his daughter's differences and beliefs cause another argument, creating more tension between them. Mr. Hoodhood does not support Bobby Kennedy, and his daughter does. He believes Bobby Kennedy is a Communist, while his daughter thinks Kennedy is the only hope for the country to restore peace and end the war in Vietnam. Mr. Hoodhood's daughter believes President Johnson resigned from the presidency because "he doesn't want to lose, not because he cares about America's future" [p. 186]. Mr. Hoodhood believes that Richard Nixon will win the election instead of Bobby Kennedy.)*

3. Why doesn't Holling's father take him to Opening Day at Yankee Stadium? How does this affect Holling? *(Holling's father views the game as unimportant. He seems disinterested when he tells Holling, "Isn't there enough happening in the world that you shouldn't have to go into the city for a baseball game" [p. 191]? Then Holling discovers his dad is busy working at the time he is supposed to take Holling to the game. Since Holling's father often puts his business and his reputation above his family, Holling is not surprised. Holling is humiliated because everyone in his class knows what happened when they see him in class after lunch recess. He thinks, "I suppose there may have been a more miserable hour sometime in my life, but I couldn't think of what it might have been" [p. 193]. Holling is disappointed because he worked diligently to finish all of his schoolwork in the morning so he could leave early for the game. He is even more disappointed because his father broke his promise to take him, even though he knew how important the game was to Holling.)*

4. How does Mrs. Baker make Holling, Danny, and Doug's experience at Yankee Stadium much more exciting? What is foreshadowed as Mrs. Baker talks with Joe Pepitone? *(Because Mrs. Baker arranged for the boys to meet some of the Yankees players one Wednesday afternoon, they recognize and acknowledge the boys and invite them onto the field. When some of the Yankees recognize Mrs. Baker from the Melbourne Olympic Games, they all gather around to talk to her and photographers take her and the boys' picture with the Yankees. Then, the Yankees give the boys a tour around the Stadium upon Mrs. Baker's request. Joe Pepitone tells Mrs. Baker the owner of*

All rights reserved

 © Novel Units, Inc.

*Yankee Stadium is looking for a classical architect to repair the stadium, and Mrs. Baker asks to meet him. This foreshadows a possible way for Mr. Kowalski to get a contract, save his business, and stay in Long Island.)*

5. How does Holling feel about the upcoming cross-country meet? Why does he stay behind the eighth graders during practice? Is he making the right choice? Why or why not? (*Holling is nervous about the meet because he doubts his abilities. He is also scared to pass the eighth graders because he knows it will anger them. Answers will vary. Some students might believe this is a wise decision that will protect Holling. Other students might think Holling is allowing the eighth graders to bully him, and as a consequence, he is not reaching his true potential.*)

6. Why does Holling decide to outrun the eighth graders during the cross-country meet? (*As Holling begins his last lap, he sees Coach Quatrini yelling for him to keep going, the Hupfers cheering him on, and Meryl Lee waving her dried rose with a ribbon. Holling might realize how important his winning is to Danny and his family since the eighth graders injured Danny and ruined his chance at winning. The biggest impetus is when Mrs. Baker commands Holling to pass the eighth graders. He says, "And that was all it took" [p. 207].*)

7. **Prediction:** What will happen to the Kowalskis?

## Supplementary Activities

1. Figurative Language: Continue adding to your figurative language chart. Examples: **Simile**—"spring break...dropped as the gentle rain from heaven upon the place beneath" (p. 198); **Metaphors**—Coach Quatrini: "pied ninny" and "blind mole" (p. 191); Holling's heartbeat: thunder (p. 205)

2. History/Writing: Research news stories from the day Martin Luther King, Jr. was assassinated. Write an essay explaining how his death affected America.

All rights reserved

## May

The junior high students practice atomic bomb drills, and Kowalski and Associates acquires the Yankee Stadium contract. Mr. Hoodhood buys a new Ford Mustang convertible. Holling's sister runs away to California with Chit. Holling's family becomes divided. Holling begins to read *The Tragedy of Hamlet, Prince of Denmark*. Holling, Meryl Lee, and Mai Thi help Danny prepare for his upcoming bar mitzvah. Mrs. Baker takes Holling on a field trip to study points of local architectural interest, and together they light a candle at Saint Adelbert's. Holling's sister calls him for help from Minneapolis, and he sends her money to get home. Meryl Lee and her father take Holling to pick up his sister from the bus station since his parents refuse to go. Mrs. Baker receives a telegram from her husband, who is alive and well.

| Vocabulary |
| --- |
| incinerated |
| rafters |
| renovate |
| extremity |
| tsar |
| synagogue |
| congregation |
| outskirts |
| abolitionist |
| incense |
| melancholy |
| combustion |

### Discussion Questions

1. What disappointments does Holling's father experience? What might his reaction to each disappointment indicate? (The Home Town Chronicle *reports that Kowalski and Associates will renovate Yankee Stadium, including the words "'Kowalski a sure bet for Chamber of Commerce Businessman of 1968'" [p. 211] in the story. In an argument between Mr. Hoodhood and his daughter over her future, she disrespects him by throwing lima beans at his model for the new junior high school. Holling's father buys a Ford Mustang convertible to comfort himself and uphold his reputation. When his daughter runs away to California with her friend Chit to "find herself," Mr. Hoodhood is angry and apathetic at first but gradually stops watering the azalea bushes [allowing them to die] and the house becomes quiet. Answers will vary. Mr. Hoodhood's reactions to the Yankee Stadium contract and his daughter leaving show he might feel inferior and out of control of both situations.)*

2. How do Meryl Lee, Mai Thi, and Holling help Danny? *(They help Danny prepare for his upcoming bar mitzvah since Danny is extremely nervous. They sacrifice their lunch recess for the majority of the month to sit inside and listen to Danny recite his service readings and encourage him when he wants to give up.)*

3. What does Holling reveal to Mrs. Baker after he asks her not to call him "Mr. Hoodhood"? How do Holling's circumstances relate to Hamlet's from the play? *(Holling confesses that he does not want to be forced to follow in his father's footsteps. He says he is afraid he "won't get the chance to see what [he] can do with the slings and arrows of outrageous fortune" [p. 220]. Mrs. Baker tells Holling that even Hamlet waited too long to do what he was passionate about.)*

4. Why do you think Mrs. Baker takes Holling to see the local architecture? *(Answers will vary. Mrs. Baker understands how Holling feels about having a predetermined future. She wants to expose him to the importance and beauty of architecture so he can see the positive aspects of the field before he dismisses it as a career. She might do this because she knows how well he can draw and she believes he has "the soul of an architect" [p. 219].)*

5. What do architecture and the atomic bomb symbolize? *(Answers will vary. Architecture is symbolic of life and historical occurrences. The atomic bomb represents war and destruction. Architecture provides foundations for life and communities, while the atomic bomb can destroy all of the community's life and history. This binary reflects the recurring theme in the novel that life and love should overcome war and destruction.)*

All rights reserved

 © Novel Units, Inc.

6. Why does Holling's sister want to return home? *(Answers will vary. Some students might think she wants to go home because she has run out of money. Other students might think it is because she misses Holling. Just as Holling realizes how much he loves her, his sister might have had the same realization. Their bond supersedes the differences between Holling's sister and her father. It is another example of how love can overpower war.)*

7. Why is it significant that Holling picks up his sister from the bus station without his parents' help? How has Holling changed since the beginning of the novel? *(Answers will vary. It shows that Holling no longer cares whether he upsets his father. He loves his sister and goes to lengths to bring her home. He even speaks out against his father and is prepared to take his brand-new car. At the beginning of the novel, Holling behaved as his father expected him to, as someone who is destined to inherit Hoodhood and Associates. Now, he makes choices for himself, aware that he, not his father, is in control of his future.)*

8. What does Holling mean when he tells his father that Heather found him? What is significant about this quote referring to Hamlet: "Or maybe he never had someone to tell him that he didn't need to find himself. He just needed to let himself be found" (p. 234)? *(Answers will vary. Holling is defending Heather and trying to shame his father. Holling may also be assuming that his sister has discovered she loves him as much as he loves her. Holling is also implying that Heather has realized how Holling is a big part of her life and her identity. The significance of the quote is that while a person may strive to understand himself or herself, that person really just needs someone else to accept him or her [e.g., Holling longs for his father to love and appreciate him regardless of whether he intends to inherit the company.].)*

9. What good news does Mrs. Baker receive? Why does she allow Holling to stay in the room when she receives this news? *(Her husband has been found, and he is coming home. Answers will vary. Holling and Mrs. Baker share a special bond since they spent so much time together during the year. Holling says, "You don't send someone away who has lit a candle with you" [p. 235].)*

10. **Prediction:** How will Danny perform at his bar mitzvah?


## Supplementary Activities

1. Figurative Language: Continue adding to your figurative language chart. Examples: **Similes**— "Smells like a brewery in this classroom…" (p. 220); "…her voice was as sad and lost as Loneliness" (p. 231); **Metaphor**—the sky: blue canvas (p. 222); **Personification**—"…tulips were standing at attention…" (p. 222).

2. Religion: Research bar mitzvahs. What is the significance of the tradition, when is it celebrated, and how is it celebrated? Write an essay based on your findings.

3. Architecture: Find a historic building in your city, and contact the Chamber of Commerce or another city office to learn the history of that building. Use your findings to make a poster or a PowerPoint presentation, including an image of the building.

All rights reserved

# June

Mrs. Baker plans a class camping trip to celebrate the end of the school year, even though she hates camping. Bobby Kennedy is assassinated. While on the camping trip, the class suffers through several fiascos, involving lost utensils, heavy rainfall, and a swarm of mosquitoes. Mrs. Bigio asks Mai Thi to live with her. Danny's bar mitzvah goes perfectly, and Holling opposes his father's idea about what it means to "become a man" (p. 260). Lieutenant Baker returns home to great fanfare.

| Vocabulary |
| --- |
| comedy |
| nomination |
| taunted |
| heaved |
| resin |
| climax |
| latrines |
| repellant |
| sponsored |
| yarmulka |

## Discussion Questions

1. Why does Mrs. Baker take her class camping even though she hates camping? *(It is tradition for Mrs. Baker to take her students camping. She has taken her students every year with her husband since she began teaching at Camillo Junior High. Holling believes she takes them this year because it's what Lieutenant Baker would have wanted, and, in her mind, keeping the same routine will ensure his quick and safe return.)*

2. Why does Holling think that the real world is sometimes like Hamlet and Bobby Kennedy? *(Answers will vary. Hamlet's character in the play is scared and angry. He isn't sure about the future, and he feels helpless to improve his situation. In everyday life, people also sometimes feel overwhelmed and do not know how to change their circumstances. Bobby Kennedy promoted a message of hope to a war-weary country. He believed there was a solution to even the most dire situations and did not appear afraid or overwhelmed, but he was assassinated before he could make a difference. In the real world, good people are often never given a chance to improve a bad situation and are not paid enough attention.)*

3. Why does the class's camping trip occur at the end of the novel? *(Answers will vary. The author might want to show the culmination of many relationships that have developed throughout the novel. He might want to show how each of these relationships has been strengthened because of people's shared experiences.)*

4. What "miracle" does Holling witness at the end of the camping trip? What does the water symbolize? *(Holling sees the majestic river water flowing toward him, and it looks like light. Answers will vary. The light is symbolic of hope for the future.)*

5. Compare and contrast Holling's and his father's perception of Danny's bar mitzvah. What happens as a result of their disagreement? Why does Holling look different to Meryl Lee? *(Answers will vary. Holling's father thinks the bar mitzvah was insignificant and possibly embarrassing for Danny. He is glad he didn't make his own son "go through something like that" [p. 260]. Holling perceives the ceremony as a meaningful rite of passage and believes Danny has become a man. Holling and his father disagree about the bar mitzvah's value and significance. Holling thinks that being a man is about more than getting a good job and providing for a family. Meryl Lee might notice the relief Holling feels from standing up to his father instead of staying quiet and letting his father tell him what to believe or feel.)*

6. How are comedies and tragedies both part of Holling's life? *(Answers will vary. Suggestions: Lieutenant Baker's survival and return home, Heather's decision to return home, Danny's successful performance at his bar mitzvah, Meryl Lee and her family staying in town, and Mrs. Bigio and Mai Thi becoming a family are all examples of happy endings. Tragedies include the assassination of Bobby Kennedy and Martin Luther King, Jr., and Holling's father's refusal to acknowledge that he is more than just an architect.)*

All rights reserved

 © Novel Units, Inc.

7. What is Mrs. Baker's prediction for Holling's future? Do you agree or disagree? *(Mrs. Baker predicts that Holling will bring "peace and wisdom" to the world because he knows about "war and folly" [p. 263]. She also thinks Holling understands the value of love—how to love, how much he is loved, and how much it hurts to lose love. Answers will vary.)*

## Supplementary Activities

1. Figurative Language: Complete your figurative language chart. Examples: **Similes**—"sparks that looked like rising stars" (p. 248); "ankles like cantaloupes and shins like watermelons" (p. 249); "The mosquitoes followed us like little airplanes" (p. 254); **Metaphors**—the river: a ribbon of light (p. 257); weight: maturity (p. 259); Meryl Lee: a jewel (p. 261); **Personification**—"…sounds of sadness creep underneath the bedroom doors and along the dark halls" (p. 240); "Each beam stabbed at the cold winds, until one by one they whimpered and died" (p. 252).

2. Genre: Define "comedy," and then write a brief essay explaining whether or not *The Wednesday Wars* can be classified as a comedy.

All rights reserved

# Post-reading Discussion Questions

1. How are the Vietnam War and Shakespeare literature important to the story? *(Answers will vary. Love and war are prominent in both Shakespeare's plays and the current events of 1967 and 1968. Presenting these two elements shows the universality of love and war and the relevance of Shakespeare in contemporary society. The Vietnam War affects many of the characters in the plot. It creates tension between Heather and her father, causes Mai Thi to be persecuted, and it strikes fear in the hearts of Mrs. Baker and Mrs. Bigio. The author also uses Shakespeare's literature to compare characters in the novel to characters in the plays. Examples: Holling and Meryl Lee are compared to Romeo and Juliet; Mr. Hoodhood is compared to Shylock.)*

2. Why is the novel titled *The Wednesday Wars*? Do you think this is a fitting title? Why or why not? *(Answers will vary. The author likely uses "Wednesday" since the novel focuses on Holling's relationship with Mrs. Baker, which is mostly developed during their Wednesday afternoon class sessions. "War" might be used because of the Vietnam War that is occurring throughout the school year and how it is affecting the characters' lives. "War" can also refer to the "personal wars" fought by Holling and his friends. Throughout the novel, Holling struggles internally when he realizes he does not want to be like his father and wants to determine his own future. Holling also has various conflicts with his classmates, Mrs. Baker, the pet rats, his father, and Heather. Other characters in the novel also experience "wars." Mrs. Baker works hard to divert her attention from the fact that her husband is declared missing during the war, Mrs. Bigio copes with the death of her husband, and Heather tries to find her identity while her father continuously demeans her beliefs and dreams. Danny is overwhelmed with the pressure he feels about not embarrassing himself at his bar mitzvah, making his family proud, and transitioning into adulthood. Mai Thi is discriminated against solely because of her ethnicity, Doug must oppose his brother in order to be a good friend, Mr. Hoodhood struggles to maintain a perfect image, business, and home, Mr. Kowalski contends with business ethics, and Meryl Lee struggles to define her relationship with Holling.)*

3. Describe Holling's relationship with his sister. Why does the author wait until the end of the novel to reveal Heather's name? *(Holling and his sister tease and annoy each other at the beginning of the novel. Although they constantly ridicule each other, there is always evidence that they love each other. Heather disapproves of Holling going to military school because she does not want to lose him. Holling saves Heather from getting hit by an out-of-control bus. Heather calls Holling instead of her parents after she runs away, and Holling becomes determined to bring her home when his parents won't help. This begins a new phase of their relationship, where they realize how much they truly love and need each other. Answers will vary. The author might reveal Heather's name at the end of the novel because the revelation gives readers a new intimacy with her character as she becomes more deeply connected to Holling. The author might also want to signify the concept of Heather being "found" since her name is mentioned after she returns from her trip to "find herself." Heather's name also reveals why Holling knew which bus station to send the money to.)*

4. Describe how Mrs. Bigio changes throughout the novel. What causes this change? *(Answers will vary. At the beginning of the novel, Mrs. Bigio seems angry and short-tempered. After her husband dies in Vietnam, she grieves deeply and takes out her anger and frustration on the students, especially Mai Thi because she is Vietnamese. After Mrs. Bigio sees how people's discrimination truly affects Mai Thi, she apologizes to Mai Thi and they form a friendship. Mrs. Bigio realizes love is more important than war and eventually views Mai Thi as an individual instead of a hateful stereotype. Some students may also speculate that Mrs. Baker caused some of the changes in Mrs. Bigio since they are close friends.)*

All rights reserved

 © Novel Units, Inc.

5. Describe Holling and his father's relationship. Will Holling inherit his father's company? Why or why not? *(Answers will vary. Holling and his father are not close. Holling obeys his father and behaves as expected because he does not want to damage his father's exemplary reputation or his company's success. Holling's father is disinterested in Holling's life unless there is a possible business opportunity involved. Holling's father is proud of the company he wants Holling to inherit and wants Holling to appreciate his work, but Holling believes his father feels forced to stay a successful architect in order to provide for his family. Holling wants to determine his own future and not feel confined to architecture if he becomes passionate about something else. At first, Holling is fearful of his father. By the end of the novel, he realizes he is capable of making his own life choices and contradicts his father for the first time. Some students might think Holling will not inherit Hoodhood and Associates because he continuously says he does not want to be an architect like his dad. Other students might think he will if he learns not to associate his father's personality with the study of architecture. If he learns how to separate the two and decides he truly enjoys architecture then he might want to inherit the company after all.)*

6. Describe Mrs. Baker's relationship with Holling. How does she affect his life? Why does she help him so much? *(Answers will vary. Mrs. Baker initially seems to resent Holling because she has to stay after school on Wednesday afternoons for just one student. After she begins to teach Holling about Shakespeare, she gets to know and understand him more. She also learns about Holling's tense relationship with his father. Mrs. Baker teaches Holling life lessons by helping him to read and understand literature, apply literature to real life, and run well. She helps Holling understand the importance of loving oneself and others. Mrs. Baker is a demanding teacher who believes in all of her students and wants the best for them. She might help Holling because she sees his desire to learn and his potential to do great things. She might believe he can affect the future in a positive way since he has seen both the effects of war and the power of love. Mrs. Baker might also help Holling because she sees his parents' lack of involvement in his life.)*

7. How are the themes of peace and harmony evidenced in the novel? *(Answers will vary. Examples: The novel shows a peaceful blending of students from different backgrounds and religions. Holling's school is accommodating toward students who are Jewish, Catholic, or Protestant. Martin Luther King, Jr.'s nonviolent protests are highlighted in the novel. Mrs. Bigio and Mai Thi reconcile. Kowalski and Associates acquires a significant architecture contract with Yankee Stadium, allowing Meryl Lee and her family to stay in town. Mrs. Baker is reunited with her husband. Heather and Holling gain a new appreciation and respect for each other.)*

8. Holling and Mrs. Baker often discuss the "quality of mercy" (p. 47). What does it mean if the quality of mercy is not strained? How do characters in the novel show mercy to one another? What message is the author trying to convey? *(If the quality of mercy is not strained, then people still have the capacity to show mercy. It can also mean mercy can be freely given; it costs nothing to show mercy. Answers will vary. Examples of merciful acts in the novel: Mrs. Baker replaces Holling's rat-eaten cream puffs with new ones. Holling sends money to his sister so she can come home and picks her up from the bus station. The bus driver gives Holling a free ride and baseball for Mickey Mantle to autograph. Holling forgives Meryl Lee after her father steals Holling's father's school design. Mr. Kowalski withdraws his bid for the contract he believes he won unfairly. The author might want to demonstrate how showing mercy and being kind to others is more beneficial than being selfish or cruel.)*

9. How does the author establish a time line for the story? Are his methods effective? Why or why not? *(The author establishes time by use of chapter headings. Each chapter chronicles a different month during the school year, making it easy for readers to follow along. The historical events happening concurrently also help the reader with time. Answers will vary.)*

All rights reserved

10. How might the story be different if written from Mrs. Baker's point of view? Why does the author write from Holling's point of view? *(Answers will vary. The story might have a more mature tone if written from Mrs. Baker's point of view since she is older and more confident, whereas Holling is still discovering who he is. The author might write from Holling's point of view so the novel's adolescent audience can relate to him. Giving insight into Holling's thoughts and beliefs also helps the readers understand him. The readers also see Holling's naiveté when he injects humor into the story.)*

11. Why does the author emphasize Mrs. Baker's pet rats in the story? *(Answers will vary. Mrs. Baker's pet rats are named Sycorax and Caliban, which are also the names of the villains in* The Tempest. *The rats are unpleasant just as the villains are. The novel does not state whether Mrs. Baker named the rats after the characters in the play, but students might think she did since she seems to like Caliban due to his ability to use defeat to grow.)*

12. What, if anything, would you change about this novel? Why? *(Answers will vary.)*

13. Research the character of Shylock in *The Merchant of Venice*. How does Shylock compare to Mr. Hoodhood? *(Answers will vary. Both characters are selfish and lose their daughters somehow. Just as Shylock loses everything in court, Mr. Hoodhood believes he has lost a contract after seeing Mr. Kowalski's proposal for the new junior high school. Both try to exert control over their lives and find they cannot control others, even their own children. They are also both controversial figures who are victims of their circumstances.)*

14. Compare and contrast Holling and Meryl Lee to Romeo and Juliet. *(Answers will vary. Meryl Lee and Holling have a love-hate relationship at the beginning of the novel, while Romeo and Juliet seem to fall in love at first sight. However, Holling's and Meryl Lee's families are in competition with each other just as Romeo's and Juliet's families are sworn enemies.)*

All rights reserved

# Post-reading Extension Activities

## Writing

1. Write a biography of Robert F. Kennedy, and cite your sources. Then, write three to four paragraphs explaining whether or not you think he would have won the presidential election and how his beliefs may have changed the United States.

2. Write an essay about the definition of a hero. Identify any characters in the novel you believe are heroes, and explain why. Give examples from the novel to support your ideas.

3. Write a poem that reflects the sentiments of many Americans in the late 1960s. If desired, read your poem aloud using background music.

## Drama

4. Working with a group, select a scene from one of Shakespeare's plays and perform it for your class. Use costumes or any other props to enhance the performance.

5. With a few of your classmates, reenact the bus scene in which Holling saves his sister from being hit. Consider what emotions and thoughts Holling might have been experiencing in this scene.

## Research

6. Research the Battle of Khe Sanh. Prepare a report answering the following questions: Why was this location strategic? What debate surrounded the decision to overtake Khe Sanh? How did military action culminate? Be sure to cite your sources.

7. Ask your teacher to invite a park ranger or an Eagle Scout to your class to give a presentation on safe camping. Be sure to prepare questions to ask the speaker during or after the presentation.

## Art

8. Design a building for a purpose of your choice. Your design should include the building's exterior and a sample of the interior.

9. Create a diorama of the "Perfect House" described in the novel.

## Government

10. Hold a "classroom leader" election with two distinct campaigns. Each student should have a specific role in the campaign. The class will vote on a winner after each candidate's campaign (complete with a slogan, advertisement, and debate or speech) has been presented.

All rights reserved

# Assessment for *The Wednesday Wars*

Assessment is an ongoing process. The following ten items can be completed during study of the novel. Once finished, the student and teacher will check the work. Points may be added to indicate the level of understanding.

Name _____ Date _____

**Student**      **Teacher**

_____      _____      1. Write a brief epilogue telling what happens during the summer after Holling's seventh-grade year.

_____      _____      2. Complete the Story Map on page 35 of this guide.

_____      _____      3. Write a character sketch for Holling. Whom would you cast to play his role in a movie, and why?

_____      _____      4. Complete the Create a Time Line activity on page 36 of this guide.

_____      _____      5. Write a summary of the novel using at least ten vocabulary words from the lists in this guide.

_____      _____      6. Complete the Character Analysis chart on page 37 of this guide.

_____      _____      7. Write a newspaper article describing a momentous event that occurred during Holling's seventh-grade year.

_____      _____      8. Complete the Sorting Characters chart on page 38 of this guide. Note that some characters may fit into more than one category.

_____      _____      9. Complete the Solving Problems chart on page 39 of this guide.

_____      _____      10. Correct any quizzes and tests taken over the novel.

All rights reserved

 © Novel Units, Inc.

# Attribute Web

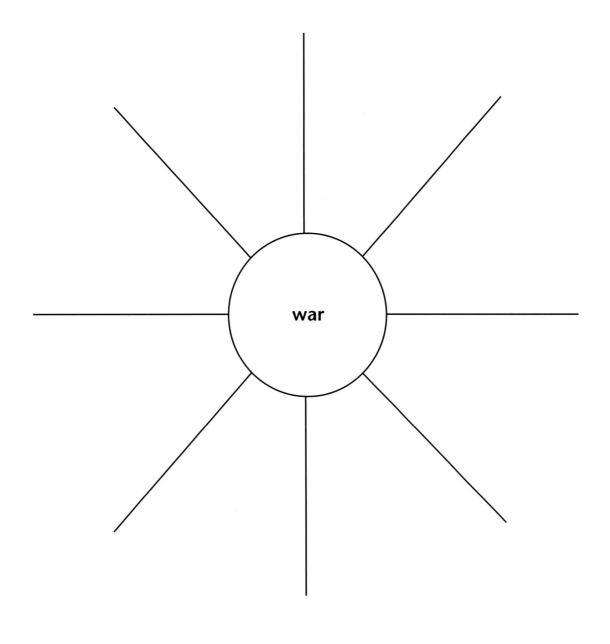

All rights reserved

# Venn Diagram

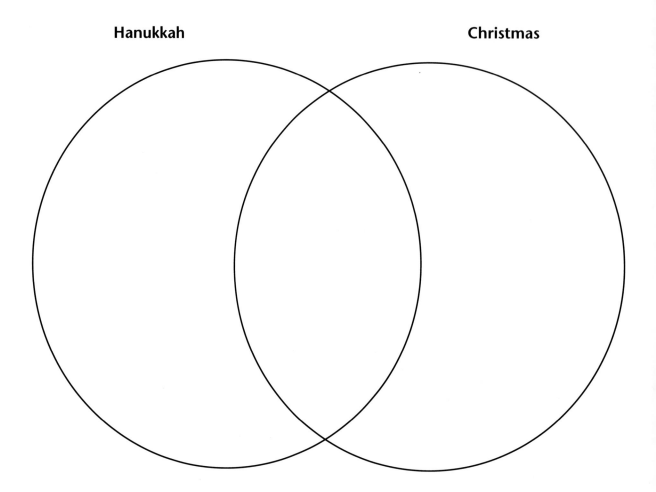

Hanukkah                                          Christmas

All rights reserved

# Story Map

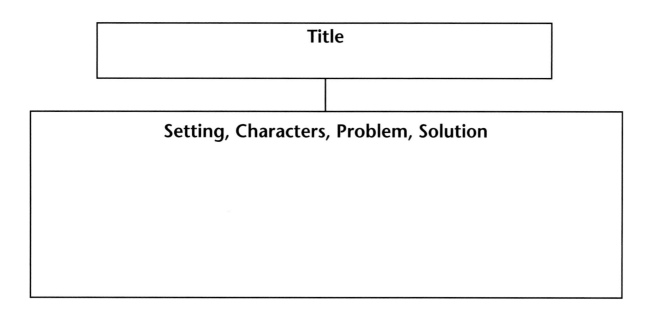

| Title |
|---|

| Setting, Characters, Problem, Solution |
|---|

**Series of Events**

All rights reserved

# Create a Time Line

**Directions:** In the numbered boxes below, illustrate major events from the novel in chronological order.

| | | |
|---|---|---|
| 1. | 2. | 3. |
| 4. | 5. | 6. |
| 7. | 8. | 9. |
| 10. | 11. | 12. |

All rights reserved

 © Novel Units, Inc.

# Character Analysis

**Directions:** Working in small groups, discuss the attributes of the various characters. In each character's box, write several words or phrases that describe him or her.

Holling

Heather

Meryl Lee

Danny Hupfer

Doug Swieteck

Mr. Hoodhood

Mrs. Baker

Mrs. Bigio

All rights reserved

# Sorting Characters

**Directions:** Similarities between characters are sometimes a clue to themes in a story. Place this novel's characters in one or more of the groups below.

| Victims | Victimizers | Fighters |
|---|---|---|
|  |  |  |
| **Peace-lovers** | **Conformists** | **Self-directors** |
|  |  |  |

All rights reserved

 © Novel Units, Inc.

# Solving Problems

**Directions:** List six problems the characters in the novel face. Then complete the rest of the chart. For each problem, circle which solution you think is best—yours or the character's.

| Problem | Character's Solution | Your Solution |
|---|---|---|
| | | |
| | | |
| | | |
| | | |
| | | |
| | | |

All rights reserved

# Linking Novel Units® Lessons to National and State Reading Assessments

During the past several years, an increasing number of students have faced some form of state-mandated competency testing in reading. Many states now administer state-developed assessments to measure the skills and knowledge emphasized in their particular reading curriculum. The discussion questions and post-reading questions in this Novel Units® Teacher Guide make excellent open-ended comprehension questions and may be used throughout the daily lessons as practice activities. The rubric below provides important information for evaluating responses to open-ended comprehension questions. Teachers may also use scoring rubrics provided for their own state's competency test.

*Please note:* The Novel Units® Student Packet contains optional open-ended questions in a format similar to many national and state reading assessments.

## Scoring Rubric for Open-Ended Items

| | |
|---|---|
| **3-Exemplary** | Thorough, complete ideas/information<br>Clear organization throughout<br>Logical reasoning/conclusions<br>Thorough understanding of reading task<br>Accurate, complete response |
| **2-Sufficient** | Many relevant ideas/pieces of information<br>Clear organization throughout most of response<br>Minor problems in logical reasoning/conclusions<br>General understanding of reading task<br>Generally accurate and complete response |
| **1-Partially Sufficient** | Minimally relevant ideas/information<br>Obvious gaps in organization<br>Obvious problems in logical reasoning/conclusions<br>Minimal understanding of reading task<br>Inaccuracies/incomplete response |
| **0-Insufficient** | Irrelevant ideas/information<br>No coherent organization<br>Major problems in logical reasoning/conclusions<br>Little or no understanding of reading task<br>Generally inaccurate/incomplete response |

All rights reserved